JEEP

Trivia & Fun Facts Every Fan Should Know About The Great American Brand!

By Rick Harper

Please consider writing a review!
Just visit: purplelink.org/review

Copyright 2021. Rick Harper.
All Rights Reserved.

Bridge Press
bp@purplelink.org

ISBN: 978-1-955149-09-9

TABLE OF CONTENTS

INTRODUCTION

Are you familiar with how and why the original Jeep was created? The Jeep brand has been around since right before the United States joined WWII. It was created in 1940 and then went into full-scale production for the US Allied forces in Europe.

The Army asked several carmakers for bids when an on-the-road wartime vehicle was needed. Only three carmakers responded. Willys-Overland was awarded the bid in July 1941 to produce 16,000 Jeeps. These Jeeps were to go to Russia and England because the US had not yet entered the war. When the United States did enter the war and used Jeep in mass, General George C. Marshall, US Army Chief of Staff during WWII, and later U.S. Secretary of State, described the Jeep Brand 4x4 as "America's greatest contribution to modern warfare."

During combat, US troops were said to have emotional bonds with their Jeeps only second to that with their rifles. The Jeep saw them through in battles and delivered what they needed regardless of the peril. Jeeps carried them safely out of harm's way and were able to be loaded with the weapons they needed to protect and serve.

This trivia book covers how the Jeep was conceived from the beginning origins of the Jeep up to what Jeep brings to the road today. A series of multiple-choice and true or false questions open each chapter, with the corresponding answers on the page after. A "Did You Know" portion consisting of interesting facts and stories closes each chapter, so you can depart that topic with a stronger connection to life of interesting facts about the Jeep brand we know today.

As you read this book, you will see how strong the Jeep community is today, even after 80 years! Jeep and the community of people who own them continue to share their love of all the Jeep vehicles in clubs and on the many trails in the US and around the world.

The information and statistics in this book are up to date as of early 2021. Jeep's history has a deep connection to us and the existence and future of Jeeps are still very much alive, as production lines continue to bring new Jeep cars, trucks, and SUVs to consumers each day!

Use this book to test your knowledge with a round of trivia on various topics and perhaps review or gain information along the way. Whether you consider yourself a die-hard expert on Jeep or are faintly familiar with WWII facts of how the Jeep came about, this book offers the opportunity to reinforce your knowledge of one of the most historic and helpful cars to ever be produced in the United States.

Let's see how much you know about Jeeps!

CHAPTER 1:

HISTORY AND ORIGINS

TRIVIA TIME!

1. What are the names of the three car companies who responded to the Army's requests for the original bids on Jeep?

   a. Chevy, Ford, Willys
   b. Ford, Willys, Dodge
   c. Willys, Bantam, Ford
   d. Dodge, Ford, Willys

2. How many models were first requested by the army to be produced?

   a. 500
   b. 10,000
   c. 25,000
   d. 16,000

3. Jeep won a medal during WWII. Which medal was given to Jeep?

   a. The Congressional Medal of Honor
   b. A Purple Heart
   c. Legion of Merit
   d. World War II Victory Medal

4. What was the first all-steel station wagon from Jeep called?

   a. Woodie
   b. Party Time
   c. The Steel Wheels
   d. Wagon Ho!

5. The improved MB Jeep could even ride on train tracks. (T/F)

6. What year did Jeep make it to the civilian lifestyle?

   a. 1945
   b. 1946
   c. 1944
   d. 1948

7. Jeep was not responsible for their famous grill on the front. Which car manufacturer was?

   a. Dodge
   b. Ford
   c. Chevy
   d. Bantam

8. What does CJ stand for?

   a. Cherokee Jeep
   b. Cheap Jeep

c. Civilian Jeep

d. Cashed-out Jeep

9. Who acquired the Jeep brand at the end of the 1960s from Willys?

   a. Ford
   b. AMC
   c. Kaiser Motors
   d. Chrysler

10. How did the name Jeep come about?

   a. Jeep stood for Joe Engineered Equipment Private.
   b. Jeep was the word that sounded like GP which was General Purpose.
   c. Jeep was the name of the auto company at the time.
   d. Jeep was named after the famous JP Morgan, due to his help with the war effort in Jeep construction. The initials JP were used and eventually the name Jeep was given.

11. The original cost per Jeep was less than $700. (T/F)

12. What delivery company bought Jeep to make their deliveries?

   a. Blue Bell Ice Cream
   b. The US Postal Service
   c. Federal Express
   d. Sees Candy

13. Beginning in 1973, all camp Jeep vehicles were equipped with AMC 304 or 360 ___ engines

   a. V6
   b. V8
   c. V4
   d. V10

14. Which decade gave Jeep its claim to fame as a vehicle of recreation?

   a. The 1960s
   b. The 1980s
   c. The 1970s
   d. The 1950s

15. In January 1975, the Chief Cherokee was introduced. At the time, what was this car most famous for?

   a. The appeal to younger, more sporty drivers
   b. The extended space between the front and back seats
   c. Being the 1st vehicle to win *Four Wheeler Magazine*'s Achievement Award
   d. The variety of colors available for the first time

16. Which President was frequently seen driving his Blue Scrambler Jeep on his own ranch?

   a. Bill Clinton
   b. George Bush Sr.
   c. George Bush Jr.
   d. Ronald Reagan

17. In 2003, Jeep introduced their latest and greatest trail vehicle Jeep ever and named it the Rubicon. It is named after a famous trail in what location?

    a. The Sierra Nevada Mountains
    b. The San Andres Mountains
    c. The Grand Canyon
    d. Yellowstone National Park

18. When Jeep first started producing trucks, who did they aim their marketing program toward?

    a. Over the road truck drivers
    b. Teenagers who love trucks
    c. Farmers and construction workers
    d. Moving companies

19. The Jeepster (VJ) was most famous for what?

    a. Being very cheap, in its day, selling for $1,900
    b. Promoted as a car mainly for men
    c. Known as a youthful and sporty car
    d. CJ vehicle with 4-wheel drive.

20. The word Jeep became a registered trademark of Willy-Overland in which year?

    a. 1950
    b. 1940
    c. 1960
    d. 1945

ANSWERS

1. C – Willys, Bantam, Ford

2. D – 16,000

3. B – A Purple Heart

4. A – Woodie

5. True

6. A – 1945

7. B – Ford

8. C – Civilian Jeep

9. C – Kaiser Motors

10. B – Jeep was the word that sounded like GP which was General Purpose

11. False

12. B – The U.S. Postal Service

13. B – V8

14. A – The 1960s

15. C – Being the 1st vehicle to win *Four Wheeler Magazine*'s Achievement Award.

16. D – Ronald Reagan

17. A – The Sierra Mountains

18. C – Farmers and construction workers

19. C – Known as a youthful and sporty car

20. A –1950

DID YOU KNOW?

- The original Jeep was designed in just two days. The idea was that our allies already in the war needed the old Model T vehicles replaced, and President Roosevelt also knew it would not be long until our troops would be joining the war effort in Europe. So, when the bids went out to design and bid the Jeep, a barely known company called Bantam designed and organized a bid which with which Willys and Ford helped them. The entire process of writing the bid and contract took place from July 14, 1941, until the contract and bid was handed to the government on July 22. The design itself was completed in 2 days.

- The Jeep underwent several improvements and rounds of testing before being released to troops during WWII. Improvements were constantly being made to each and every prototype. Every improvement made vast differences in capabilities and efficiency. The bombing of Pearl Harbor escalated the speed at which Jeeps were produced. Willys and Ford produced a Jeep every 90 seconds during the war.

- No one imagined the way Jeeps would be used during the war. The commanders used the hoods to lay down maps and plans when talking with troops, and they heated rations on the hoods as well in the cans. Troops also used the hot water drips from the radiators as liquid for shaving.

- Jeeps were modified in order to use in the desert and on the beach during the Normandy invasion. Jeeps were the perfect size to load in airplanes then put in gliders so they could land for the D-Day invasion. Jeeps were modified to have snowplows on the front, to be used as ambulances and fire trucks, to lay phone cable, and to be operated as generators. With the correct wheels, the Jeep could also be a small train engine.

- In the Jeep's first public outing in the United States, the driver was asked what the vehicle was, and he said, "It's a Jeep!" After that, he promptly drove up the Capitol steps to demonstrate what a Jeep could do!

- In 2016, The Jeep Grand Cherokee was named the 2016 Most Popular Midsize SUV on Edmonds.Com.

- Jeep's slogan is: Do Anything.® This is a way of life, not just a slogan. The Jeep badge stands for more than a brand. In truth, it's a badge of honor.

- The all-purpose MB was amazingly versatile. It could be fitted with .30 or .50 caliber machine guns for combat. It was also widely modified for long-range desert patrol, snow plowing, telephone cable laying, sawmilling, as a firefighting pumper, field ambulance, tractor, and, with suitable wheels, to even run on railway tracks.

- A nonprofit organization in Toledo, Ohio says it will open a 56,000-square-foot interactive Jeep museum in 2022 that is expected to draw about 250,000 visitors annually. If you already didn't know, Toledo is where the very first Jeeps were manufactured.

- The M38 served in the Korean War and was seen in nearly every episode of the TV series M*A*S*H.

- In 1962, the first automatic transmission and independent suspension were placed in the Jeep Wagoneer.

- Willys Motors introduced the Fleetvan (FJ-3/FJ-3A) for delivery vehicles. We still see some rendition of those vehicles today. Every time you see a postal truck, Amazon delivery vehicle, Fed Ex, or any number of other vehicles where the driver is able to exit from the right side to make deliveries to the right side of the street, it all traces back to the Willys Motors and Jeep.

- A scam to civilians during WWII was run in *Boys' Life* and *Popular Science* magazines advertising for Jeeps in a crate for only $50. Of course, all the person who wanted the Jeep had to do was to send in $20 ($200 in today's money), and the Jeep would be sent to the buyer in a crate. There were actually Jeeps in crates, but these Jeeps were sent to our allies, such as England. There are no records of anyone receiving one of these Jeeps in crates. These Jeeps were supposed to be surplus goods, and the ads even wanted people to send in ideas about how they were going to use the surplus goods after they received them. The pictures they used of the Jeeps in crates were, of course, on their way to Europe for the war.

- During WWII, Jeeps traveled up to 45 mph, which was good for the time in the battle zone. Often used for transporting people and supplies, as well as the wounded, the Jeep had a three-speed transmission with three gears and reverse. The engine was able to produce 60 horsepower at 4000 RPM, which was also good for the standards of the time. Willys's Jeep had four-wheel drive as well.

- Jeep was credited with being another soldier on the field. Jeep cannot be stressed enough as being essential to soldiers in WWII. During the war, Jeeps were manufactured at one Jeep per minute by both Ford and Willys and sent overseas. Soldiers used these Jeeps literally as a tool for things the creators could not imagine, such as heating rations on the hood, putting windshields down to make it easier to shoot larger weapons, using the hood to plan strategies, and more. The Jeep was the US soldier's partner in battle and camp.

CHAPTER 2:

PEOPLE INVOLVED WITH JEEP

1. Who designed the first Jeep in less than two days?
   a. Henry Ford
   b. Winston Churchill
   c. Karl K. Probst
   d. Willys

2. Who was Eugene the Jeep?
   a. A little Jeep in a cartoon
   b. A doglike character on Popeye
   c. A little Jeep on Mickey Mouse
   d. A nickname for the first Jeep model

3. Who was president of the United States when the government requested the vehicle that was eventually called the Jeep to be made?
   a. Franklin Roosevelt
   b. Teddy Roosevelt
   c. Woodrow Wilson
   d. Dwight D. Eisenhower

4. Joseph Frazier from Chrysler joined John Willy at Willys-Overland in _____, not knowing the chance that Willys-Overland would have just three years later!

   a. 1940

   b. 1939

   c. 1938

   d. 1941

5. The exterior of the 2018 model of this Jeep was designed by Taylor Langhals.

   a. Cherokee Chief

   b. Gladiator

   c. Grand Wagoneer

   d. Wrangler

6. Elizabeth Krear is a mechanical engineer who worked on both the Gladiator and the Jeep Comanche Truck. (T/F)

7. Ernie Pyle, famed WWII correspondent, said this about the Jeep in 1943: "It's…"

   a. Faithful as a dog

   b. Agile as a goat

   c. Strong as a mule

   d. All of the above

8. The new global president of Jeep is Christian Meunier. Why is that important? (Choose 2)

a. The Jeep will keep pushing further than North America.
b. The Jeep brand will see less action in North America.
c. Jeep will build some variants of Jeep the North American market will not see.
d. Jeep will cut back on the Cherokee.

9. The oldest surviving Jeep of WWII is known by the name _____ and lives in the Smithsonian Institute.

   a. Eugene
   b. GP
   c. Gramps
   d. Lucky

10. What general rode in the most Jeeps and later became president?

    a. General Ford
    b. General George W. Bush
    c. General Dwight D Eisenhower
    d. General Patton

11. Mark A. Smith organized the first Jeep Trek across the Rubicon Trail in 1953 near this city.

    a. Tahoe
    b. Reno
    c. Las Vegas
    d. Carson City

12. The man who designed the "Easter egg" phenomenon in the Jeep since 1996 is designer Michael Santoro. What is it?

    a. A hidden egg under each grill
    b. An animal or message somewhere on or inside the car
    c. An egg under the windshield wipers
    d. A hidden message under the wheels

13. In the early 60s when Willys had financial difficulty, Jeep was sold to:

    a. Henry J. Kaiser
    b. Henry Ford Jr.
    c. Walter Chrysler
    d. David Buick

14. Which name is the first name of the owner of Willys?

    a. Don
    b. Frank
    c. Hank
    d. John

15. Barney Roos started working for Willys in 1938 and was chief engineer for the Go Devil engine in the Jeep. (T/F)

16. Enzo Ferrari once said, "Jeep is America's only real sports car." Which American car company was he insulting at the time?

a. Chevy
b. Ford
c. Buick
d. Chrysler

17. The former president of Willys-Overland, Joe Frazier said that Jeep actually got its name from slurring the letters GP together. GP stands for General Purpose. (T/F)

18. Which country in Europe gave Dwight D. Eisenhower a Jeep and a castle apartment in 1946 just after WWII?

a. England
b. Scotland
c. Austria
d. France

19. Who was the designer that made the Woodie station wagon affordable and more attractive for consumers in 1946?

a. Brooks Stevens
b. John Willys
c. Elizabeth Krear
d. Karl Probst

20. Jeep has a long list of Jeep founders. Which person does not belong on this list?

a. Delmar Roos
b. Charles Probst
c. Col. William F. Lee

d. Henry Ford

ANSWERS

1. C – Karl K Probst

2. B –A doglike character on Popeye

3. A – Franklin Roosevelt

4. C – 1938

5. B – Gladiator

6. True

7. D – All of the above

8. A and C – The Jeep will keep pushing further than North America, and Jeep will build some variants of Jeep the North American market will not see.

9. C – Gramps

10. C – General Dwight D. Eisenhower

11. A – Tahoe

12. B – An animal or message somewhere on or inside the car

13. A – Henry J Kaiser

14. D – John

15. True

16. A – Chevy

17. True

18. B – Scotland

19. A – Brooks Stevens

20. D – Henry Ford

DID YOU KNOW?

- Mark Smith died when he was 87, but fans of Jeeps all over the world give Smith the credit for creating the sport of off-road trekking in a community. Mark Smith founded the JJUSA for this community in 1982. This organization offers over 100 off-road trips every year for Jeep enthusiasts. Without Mr. Smith, it probably would have taken much longer for the crowd of Jeep owners to come together, but because of Mark Smith, people from all over the world feel like when they purchase a Jeep, they are also becoming members of a larger club of people. Beginners and veterans alike go on different off-road trips every year along with their families and friends to enjoy the full capacities of the Jeep experience.

- Michael Santoro began the design of hiding Easter eggs in every Jeep in 1996. These Easter eggs are somewhere in almost every single Jeep since that date. If you are a Jeep owner, look for your symbol, animal, or message hidden usually in plain sight. There are several TikTok videos about the Easter eggs.

- Some Jeeps have several Easter eggs, and they are in very random places. As the newer Jeeps are produced, the Easter eggs have become even more symbolic in nature, and some eggs are just for plain old-fashioned fun, like the Jeep itself!

- So many people came together for the Jeep to be the vehicle it became for the war effort. Karl Probst designed the prototype for the vehicle. Delmar "Barney" Roos beefed up the engine to its Go Devil capacity. Other designers, as well, had input by the time Jeep hit the ground in Europe.

- Car designers and engineers with these companies also contributed to Jeep models over the years: Willys-Overland, Kaiser Jeep, American Motors, Renault, Chrysler, DaimlerChrysler, Cerberus Capital Management, Fiat Chrysler Automobiles.

- Elizabeth Krear is the engineer behind the Jeep model rugged truck as well as the Gladiator. While she loves the trucks, she said engineering the Gladiator was her proudest accomplishment on the Jeep line. To begin with, Gladiator is a truck, and one of the most attractive features for people who have purchased the Gladiator is the shorter bed. This Gladiator was designed with a longer wheelbase and rear suspension which is comparable with a 1500 Ram truck.

- Franklin Roosevelt spoke with General Patton in Casablanca from the passenger seat of a Jeep while Patton stood at attention to listen to his Commander-in-Chief.

- Gramps, the oldest Jeep, is in the Smithsonian. This Jeep survived WWII. It is in the "We Can Do It!" display in the Natural Museum of American History.

- Many car companies and their owners lost money or were on the verge of bankruptcy over the years from the 1930s to the present. But through it all, Jeep survived being bought and sold several times. No matter who owns Jeep, the brand remains popular and strong.

CHAPTER 3:

JEEPS IN MOVIES AND TV

1. What color were the Jeeps in Jurassic Park?

    a. Green
    b. Gray
    c. Red
    d. Yellow

2. What was the name of the Jeep that Daisy Duke had painted on the door of her CJ-7 on *Dukes of Hazzard*?

    a. Daisy 2
    b. Diva
    c. Drives
    d. Dixie

3. Marty McFly catches a ride on the back of a CJ-7 in *Back to the Future II* riding a

    a. Hovercraft
    b. Skateboard
    c. Horse
    d. Bicycle

4. What tropical show also featured a Jeep for tourists to ride to their quarters?

   a. *Hawaii 5-0*
   b. *Fantasy Island*
   c. *Loveboat*
   d. *Gilligan's Island*

5. What is the name of the Jeep in the movie *Cars*?

   a. Captain
   b. Private
   c. Sarge
   d. General

6. Four women played in a 1944 movie starring Martha Raye using an authentic Willy Jeep. The title of this movie is:

   a. Four Jills and a Jeep
   b. Jeep, Jeep, we all Sing Jeep
   c. Hey, There Where is Your Jeep?
   d. Four Jeeps for Me

7. What Jeep does Skyler White drive in *Breaking Bad*?

   a. Wrangler
   b. Cherokee
   c. Grand Wagoneer
   d. Commander

8. You will never see any Jeeps driven in *Walking Dead*. (T/F)

9. Which Jeep is driven in the 90's film *Clueless*?

a. Wrangler
b. Cherokee
c. Gladiator
d. Commander

10. The Fratelli Gang in 1984's *Goonies* had a shootout and car chase at the beginning of the film. They were in a Jeep Commander (T/F)

11. If you have watched *Twister*, then you know what Jo drove before the scene when her Jeep gets lifted off the ground. Which model was her Jeep?

a. Gladiator
b. Cherokee
c. Comanche
d. Renegade

12. Who was in love with their Jeep Wrangler and would go to the far reaches to keep it alive?

a. Daisy Duke (*Dukes of Hazzard*)
b. Lorelei Gilmore (*Gilmore Girls*)
c. Emma Peele (*Avengers*)
d. Sabrina (*Charlie's Angels*)

13. In the movie *Forrest Gump*, the Jeep shows up in Vietnam and also when Forrest is growing up as a young man. (T/F)

14. Lara Croft in the *Tomb Raider* sequel traded in her Land Rover Defender for a

a. Wrangler Rubicon

b. Gladiator
c. Renegade
d. Compass

15. *Band of Brothers* was a mini-series on HBO and featured countless Willys during the filming. What decade was it released?

    a. 1990 - 1999
    b. 2010 - 2019
    c. 1980 - 1989
    d. 2000 - 2009

16. Even in the cartoon, Beavis and Butthead drove a Jeep. It was a Jeep Cherokee. What color was it?

    a. Red
    b. Yellow
    c. Black
    d. Green

17. What was written on the Jeep Gumby and Pokey used in the old 1957-1967 show, *Gumby*?

    a. Yellow Jeep
    b. Pokey's
    c. Sparky
    d. Gumby's Jeep

18. About how many Jeeps were used in the making of *Band of Brothers*?

    a. 600 - 1000
    b. 500 - 600

c. 200 - 400
d. 100 - 200

ANSWERS

1. B – Gray

2. D – Dixie

3. A – Hovercraft

4. B – Fantasy Island

5. D – General

6. A – Four Jills and a Jeep

7. C – Grand Wagoneer

8. False

9. A – Wrangler

10. False – a Cherokee XJ

11. C – Comanche

12. B – Lorelei Gilmore (*Gilmore Girls*)

13. True

14. A – Wrangler Rubicon

15. D – 2000 - 2010

16. A – Red

17. D – Gumby's Jeep

18. A – 600 - 1000 Jeeps

DID YOU KNOW?

- The creators of *Band of Brothers* wanted to be as accurate as possible when depicting World War II scenes, so that is why they used so many Willys Jeeps to make the HBO movie series.

- Chrysler spent $10 million for the Jeep promotion during their 60th anniversary that was celebrated during the release of *Band of Brothers*, and HBO spent another 15 million on the Jeeps they used for the movie. The series won multiple awards and is still running today, 20 years later.

- When Marty McFly was supposedly following a Wrangler YJ in *Back to the Future II*, the ironic thing is that the Wrangler YJ was no longer used in the year 2015 when he was supposedly riding behind it.

- Lara Croft's Rubicon had 35-inch tires and was fully set to do every stunt in the movie *Tomb Raider*.

- Not only was Elvis photographed in his Jeep driving and riding in the Korean War, but he was also photographed working on his Jeep in cameo shots as well. You will not find too many photos of Elvis in Korea. He accepted his draft notice and went to war without any special treatment. He was a regular GI and began his service in 1958. He did have an initial deferment in order to finish filming a movie, but immediately after filming, Elvis went to Ft. Chaffee.

- Just as Elvis was able to work on his Jeep, all soldiers took pride in being able to make minor repairs on their Jeeps. The Jeep is one vehicle that is easy for owners to work on, which is why soldiers felt a kinship to their Jeeps. They could quickly fix the small troubles that might arise. There is just a special bond between a car and the driver when you are able to work on that car.

- There were a host of Jeeps used at various times during the filming of the *Walking Dead*. Anytime characters could get a Jeep started along the road, they used it! Of course, because the characters were going through many mishaps and rugged territory, the Jeeps were used by the producers.

- *Fantasy Island*'s blue tourist Jeep is on display in Hawaii on the Island of Maui at the Hotel Wailea.

- Tom Hanks and Steven Spielberg both worked on *Band of Brothers* and *Saving Private Ryan*. While hundreds of Jeeps were used in *Band of Brothers*, not one Jeep was used in *Saving Private Ryan*, except during a cut scene.

- John Wayne's legs were reportedly almost too long for the Willys Jeep. Regardless, he rode in several during the filming of many movies over his career.

CHAPTER 4:

MORE FAMOUS PEOPLE AND JEEPS

1. Which singer had his photo taken in the Jeep during the Korean War?

    a. Bob Hope
    b. Janis Joplin
    c. Elvis
    d. Bing Crosby

2. Ronald Reagan owned not one but two Jeeps and used them on his ranch. What were they? (Pick two)

    a. CJ -8 Scrambler
    b. Cherokee Chief
    c. Willys CJ - 6
    d. Wrangler

3. Harrison Ford drives a Jeep Liberty wrapped in what?

    a. *Star Wars*-themed décor
    b. Star spangled banner pattern

c. Indiana Jones Jeep pattern

d. Camouflage

4. Which actor rode in the most Jeeps on TV and in the movies?

   a. John Wayne
   b. Jimmy Stewart
   c. Tom Hanks
   d. Alan Alda

5. Roy Roger's iconic Jeep was named

   a. Bullet
   b. Belle
   c. Nellybelle
   d. Trigger

6. David Beckham surprised fans after he moved to the United States when he picked his son up from school in a

   a. Jeep Grand Cherokee
   b. Rolls Royce
   c. Jeep Wrangler
   d. Lamborghini

7. Tim McGraw and Faith Hill have several Jeeps. Their favorite is a C J-6 Rubicon they borrowed to go on a date. Faith Hill later bought that same Jeep for Tim's birthday. The color of this special Jeep is:

   a. Blue
   b. Purple

c. Multi-colored
d. Red

8. Actress Amber Rose had a custom chrome wrap with wheels to match that was what color?

   a. Aqua
   b. Pink
   c. Purple
   d. Pearl

9. When Usher had his Jeep Wrangler Rubicon modified, he did what?

   a. Lifted the suspension 3 inches
   b. Increased wheel size 5 inches
   c. Ordered dark purple chrome wrap
   d. Modified the grill

10. LeBron James has a gold custom Jeep Wrangler. (T/F)

11. Why would Blake Anderson's Jeep make any patriot jealous?

    a. His Jeep has the United States Constitution on the side.
    b. His Jeep is wrapped in the Statue of Liberty.
    c. His Jeep has an eagle and an American flag.
    d. His Jeep has Mount Rushmore on the side.

12. Floyd Mayweather drives his custom Jeep all over the off-road area around:

    a. Los Angeles

b. Las Vegas

c. Salt Lake City

d. Phoenix

13. Kim Kardashian drives a Jeep Wrangler in the Wyoming Wilderness where she and her family live. What color is her Jeep?

   a. Red

   b. Pink

   c. Black

   d. Gray

14. During Pope Francis's visit to the United States in 2015, he rode in a modified Jeep Wrangler in motorcades in both New York City and Washington D.C. (T/F)

15. Rhythm and Blues singer Chris Brown owns not one but two custom Wranglers. One of which is the iconic color of:

   a. Lime green

   b. Neon orange

   c. Neon pink

   d. Lemon yellow

16. Who gave Ronald Reagan one of his beloved Jeeps?

   a. His kids

   b. Gerald Ford

   c. Nancy Reagan

   d. George Bush Sr.

17. Elvis bought three Jeeps after returning home from the Korean War. (T/F)

18. How long did it take Jeep to talk "The Boss" into making a commercial for them?

    a. 6 months
    b. 10 months
    c. 10 years
    d. 5 years

19. J.D. Salinger was in WWII. After the war, he bought and drove an old Jeep and pretty much stayed away from crowds. He wrote a famous novel called:

    a. *From Here to Eternity*
    b. *The Grapes of Wrath*
    c. *The Catcher in the Rye*
    d. *Not Today*

20. Jeeps appeared in James Bond movies such as *Goldfinger*. (T/F)

ANSWERS

1. C – Elvis

2. A and C – CJ-8 Scrambler and Willys CJ - 6

3. B – Star spangled banner pattern

4. D – Alan Alda

5. C – Nellybelle

6. C – Wrangler

7. D – Red

8. B – Pink

9. A – Lifted the suspension 3 inches

10. True

11. C – His Jeep has an eagle and an American flag.

12. B – Las Vegas

13. C – Black

14. True

15. A – Lime green

16. C – Nancy Reagan

17. False

18. C – Ten years

19. C – *The Catcher in the Rye*

20. True

DID YOU KNOW?

- Jeep is a sponsor for Tim McGraw and Faith Hill's national tours. The couple owns several Jeeps that they use on their Nashville farm. One such Jeep was auctioned off to support their foundation for charity. They continue to drive their original red Jeep that Faith Hill bought Tim for his birthday years ago every year to celebrate their anniversaries.

- Who knew that Roy Rogers had a pet Jeep? Nellybelle was on his show for 7 years. The Jeep was often driven by his television sidekick, Pat Brady, on the ranch. He would beg the Jeep to start and then yell at the Jeep to slow down saying, "Whoa, Nellybelle!" Supposedly this Jeep was grouchy and often unpredictable. But Roy Rogers sure loved his Nellybelle. She was auctioned twice. The first time was for $110,000, and the second time was for $30,000.

- While Alan Alda barely beat out John Wayne for riding in the most Jeeps, John Wayne rode in many Jeeps in his career. While John Wayne wasn't extremely tall, he did have long legs, and this made riding in the Willys a little more difficult.

- Ronald Reagan may win the prize for being the former president who loved the Jeeps the most, and his wife Nancy was not far behind. It was said she had a poster of the famous Daisy Duke Jeep as well. Nancy and Ronnie rode Jeeps often on their ranch in California.

- Many of the Jeep colors such as lime green, hot pink, and neon yellow are only available in custom Jeeps. But for a price, you can get the color you want. For example, Amber Rose has a bright pink-wrapped Jeep and Chris Brown has a lime green model.

- Elvis did not buy any Jeeps after coming home from the Korean War. His cars are on display in Memphis, Tennessee.

- A famous person we left out of the quiz is the famous Barbie doll. For years, Barbie and Ken have both driven the Jeep Wrangler in many colors and styles, usuall']y with the top off and just a roll bar. If a Barbie doll is in the house, you can bet a Jeep Wrangler is in the house as well!

- Of course, every owner and designer of Jeep in each phase of the history of Jeep has a personal Jeep they drive.

CHAPTER 5:

FUN QUESTIONS ABOUT JEEP

1. What famous singer did a commercial in Kansas featuring his own Jeep in Super Bowl LV?

    a. Garth Brooks
    b. Ed Sheeran
    c. Bruce Springsteen
    d. Bruno Mars

2. There are eight base models of Jeep in 2021. (T/F)

3. One of the differences between the Cherokee and the Grand Cherokee is:

    a. The Cherokee comes in more colors.
    b. The Cherokee has thinner, slanted headlights.
    c. The Grand Cherokee has a different floorboard.
    d. The Grand Cherokee has thinner, more slanted headlights.

4. The Jeep with the most off-road capabilities is:

    a. Wrangler Rubicon
    b. Compass

c. Patriot

d. Renegade

5. How many slots did the front grill originally have?

   a. 6

   b. 7

   c. 13

   d. 9

6. The Rubicon is a Jeep named for the new Wrangler. It is named after

   a. The Rubicon Valley

   b. The Rubicon Trail

   c. The Rubicon Desert

   d. The Rubicon River

7. Where are most Jeeps produced?

   a. Kansas City, Missouri

   b. Brazil

   c. Toledo, Ohio

   d. Detroit, Michigan

8. What is the "Jeep wave"?

   a. A distant wave in the ocean

   b. When two Jeep drivers pass on the road and they wave

   c. When two Jeep drivers come to a stop and they sit and wave

   d. When driving along the ocean, the waves hit the side of the Jeep

9. What catalog company used to sell parts to fix the Jeep in the mid-60s?

    a. JC Penny
    b. Chrysler
    c. Montgomery Ward
    d. Sears Roebuck & Co

10. What is a special day each year for Jeep enthusiasts?

    a. April 4
    b. July 4
    c. August 4
    d. June 4

11. What model of Jeeps are the only remaining model with removable doors?

    a. Cherokee
    b. Wrangler
    c. Commander
    d. Renegade

12. The most popular Jeep vehicle today is:

    a. Cherokee
    b. Renegade
    c. Wrangler
    d. Commander

13. At the time of WWII, the Jeep weighed about _____ pounds.

    a. 2000

b. 3000

c. 1500

d. 4000

14. Which Jeep was the first Jeep to be rated a seven-passenger Jeep?

    a. Cherokee
    b. Grand Cherokee
    c. Renegade
    d. Commander

15. Jeep has been named the "Car of America." (T/F)

16. Who is Old Faithful?

    a. A geyser in Yellowstone
    b. The Jeep that won a Purple Heart in WWII
    c. The Jeep that traveled the furthest in WWII
    d. The Jeep that served in both WWII and the Korean War.

17. The year 2021 marks what anniversary for Jeep?

    a. 75 years
    b. 90 years
    c. 80 years
    d. 100 years

18. Which Jeep is now the largest Jeep model?

    a. Renegade
    b. Grand Cherokee
    c. Cherokee
    d. Commander

19. Jeep enthusiasts publicize _____ trail rides every year.

   a. Hundreds
   b. Thousands
   c. Dozens
   d. Between 1 and 100

ANSWERS

1. C - Bruce Springsteen

2. True

3. B - The Cherokee has thinner, slanted headlights.

4. A - Wrangler Rubicon

5. C - 13

6. B - Rubicon Trail

7. C - Toledo, Ohio

8. B - When two Jeep drivers pass on the road, they wave.

9. D - Sears Roebuck & Co

10. A - April 4 (4/4) 4x4

11. B - Wrangler

12. C - Wrangler

13. A - 2000

14. D - Commander

15. True

16. B - The Jeep that won a Purple Heart in WWII

17. C - 80 years

18. B - Grand Cherokee

19. B - Thousands

DID YOU KNOW?

- The front grill of the Jeep was designed for Ford originally. It did have thirteen slots in 1940. Then, in 1941, the number went down to nine. Finally, the magic number seven was finalized for the Jeep and still stands. When Willys tried to copyright the grill with nine slots, they realized Ford had already done so, so that is actually why Willys dropped down to the magic number seven. There is a legend that also says the reason why Jeep has seven slots on the grill is that the Jeep is the first vehicle to drive on every continent and each slot represents one of the seven continents, but this is just a story.

- Jeep and Hummer actually had a legal fight over the seven-slot grill on the front of the vehicles. Hummer won the suit, but Jeep also won the battle and the seven slots remain with both Jeep and Hummer. At one time, Jeep and Hummer were connected, so the high court ruled that Hummer did not steal anything from Jeep. The shared history negated the lawsuit. Hummer is built by GMC.

- One has to wonder, which car company does not have a shared history with Jeep? You only have to look across the American-made models to see that many auto manufacturers have owned Jeep or have been a part of Jeep design or production. This is in part why Jeep is the American model. People see Jeep and they see an American car.

- In the beginning, Jeep had a black widow history of killing off its owner. Jeep would be sold to a new owner just before the previous owner would go belly up. This happened over and over, and each time, Jeep would survive and move on until being owned by various divisions of Chrysler Motors.

- Jeep is known for being the leader in off-road vehicles. The Rubicon was finally named, after months of brainstorming, after the Rubicon Trail. This trail is difficult and is already an official ride for August 2021. The Jeep Wrangler Rubicon was named after the Rubicon Trail because of its off-road capabilities. The Rubicon Trail has an official rating of a 10. The Wrangler Rubicon is an off-road vehicle that can handle the most difficult off-road conditions.

- Jeep celebrated its 75th anniversary by opening the first-ever pop-up dealership in Great Britain's North York Moors National Park. The unique aspect of this dealership is that it was built along the cliff's edge and can only be reached using a 4x4 vehicle.

- In June 2017, the Jeep Cherokee and Jeep Wrangler finished first and second in the Cars.com

"American-Made" index, finishing with the most American aspects of where the car and parts were actually built. This, and the fact the Jeep was the vehicle of WWII, is the reason Jeep is the American Car.

- Old Faithful is the Jeep that won the Purple Heart. This Jeep survived Operation Watchtower in Guadalcanal and Operation Cherry Blossom in Bougainville. During those times, the Jeep received two holes in the windshield from a battleship. Old Faithful was retired in 1943.

- When Kaiser owned Jeep from 1955 to 1983, they produced 600,000 CJ 5 during that time. Even though Kaiser began to struggle, Jeep was thriving and was bought by AMC in 1970.

- Even though Jeeps are made in America, Jeep does have 10 plants in six other countries. Jeep also sells to over 140 countries worldwide. The manufacturing plants are located in the United States, Mexico, Brazil, Italy, China, and India.

- In 2016, Jeep created a special day for 4x4. This was to celebrate driving on roads less traveled. It only made sense to make this day on April 4 every year. 4/4. (4x4) Every year on April 4, Jeep and Jeep owners go to social media to share the celebration with fans using the hashtag #Jeep4x4Day. The first 4x4 Day happened in April 2016. No matter where Jeep lovers are located, on April 4th, they celebrate in their own way and then share on social media. For instance, they plan a day of off-roading or a weekend just to show love for their Jeep and the people they share their Jeep with every day.

- Some still are not sure how to pronounce the name Willys. Even though John Willys created a very successful brand, many people still pronounce his name Willies, when in fact it is Willis.

- Have you ever been on a Jeep tour? If you are a seasoned Jeep owner, then you probably haven't. But for those just thinking about buying a Jeep and wanting to test drive one to find out what the Jeep experience is all about, Jeep and adventure lovers offer tours all over the country. One such tour is called the Cuvee in Colorado. This tour takes you into the backcountry. You get a chance to drive a Jeep and follow others on back roads into a beautiful Colorado wilderness into an area you would not see from the highway. Each tour goes up in altitude and will end at a local brewery for food and drinks. Tour guides have stated that this ride has sent countless people to Jeep dealerships. They joke that they never get a commission for sales.

- There was once a sports car built by Jeep called the XJ-002. It was built on Jeep chassis, and Kaiser was the owner at the time. The car was displayed at the NYC auto show. AMC bought Jeep between the show and production of the sports car, and this car never went into mass production. It did not have the seven-slot grill.

- Since 2018, Jeep sells almost 2 million Jeeps each year.

CHAPTER 6:

JEEP JAMBOREE

1. Jeep Jamboree started because people wanted to:
    a. Ride the Rubicon trail and see how fun it would be in a Jeep.
    b. Ride into Las Vegas from Lake Tahoe on the Rubicon Trail.
    c. Ride to the Georgetown Divide area to increase the economy there.
    d. Practice riding for a bigger ride.

2. The first Jeep Jamboree was held in which year?
    a. 1963
    b. 1953
    c. 1943
    d. 1973

3. Jeepers who partake in Jeep Jamborees look at the yearly event as a
    a. Lifestyle
    b. Job
    c. Travel zone
    d. Yearly event

4. The first Jeep Jamboree had _____ Jeeps.

    a. Over 100
    b. 25
    c. 75
    d. 55

5. The Rubicon Jamboree crosses which mountain range?

    a. The Sierra Nevada Range
    b. The Rocky Mountains
    c. The San Andreas Mountains
    d. The West Elk Range

6. Jeep Jamboree trail ratings from 1 to 10 tell you how hard the navigation is on each trail. The Rubicon trail has a trail rating of:

    a. 8
    b. 1-2
    c. 9-10
    d. 6-7

7. There are over 100 Jeep Jamborees Today in the United States. (T/F)

8. Who is the founder of the Jeep Jamboree?

    a. Pearse Umlauf
    b. Mark Smith
    c. Jake Horn
    d. Jill Smith

9. You must have the following to participate in Jeep Jamborees

    a. Tow points
    b. GMRS radio
    c. Full-size spare tire
    d. All of the above

10. The Rubicon Jeep Jamboree requires which vehicle for this trail?

    a. Rubicon
    b. Comanche
    c. Cherokee
    d. Wrangler

11. Choose the best reason why the trails have ratings.

    a. To help drivers test their skills on tougher trails
    b. To tell drivers if their Jeep vehicles qualify for the trails
    c. To tell drivers the scale of scenery along the trail
    d. To tell drivers the length of the trail

12. You may have up to ___ servings of alcohol per passenger while riding on a trail during a Jeep Jamboree.

    a. 3
    b. 2
    c. 0
    d. 1

13. What is the Jeepers Jamboree?

    a. A Halloween event actually called Jeepers Creepers
    b. A larger Jamboree for all Jeep owners
    c. A more adult version of the Rubicon Trail Jamboree
    d. An East coast Jamboree for Jeep owners

14. Less than a dozen Jeep Jamborees are still open for registration and/or waitlists. (T/F)

15. Most Classic Jamboree entry fees include permits, land use fees, guides, and:

    a. Meals
    b. Lodging
    c. Extra equipment
    d. All of the above

16. What is the pet policy on Jeep Jamborees?

    a. Pets are allowed where you go on a leash.
    b. Pets are highly discouraged at Jeep Jamborees.
    c. Pets are most welcome at Jeep Jamborees.
    d. Pets are to stay with you in the dining areas.

17. The tire size for most Jeep Jamborees is:

    a. No tires larger than 40"
    b. No tires larger than 35"
    c. Tires should be 35" or smaller
    d. Tires should be a standard 33"

18. Most Jeep Jamborees are family-type events. (T/F)

19. Can a friend who owns a Toyota participate in a Jeep Jamboree?

    a. If their tire size is appropriate
    b. If they pay the entry fee
    c. If they can put the tow straps and suspension lifts on their vehicle
    d. If they ride in your Jeep

20. The cutoff date for Jamboree registrations, additions, or changes of passengers is:

    a. One month prior to the event
    b. Twenty days prior to the event
    c. Ten days prior to the event
    d. Cancellations are allowed on a case-by-case basis

ANSWERS

1. C – Ride to the Georgetown Divide area to increase the economy there

2. B – 1953

3. A – Lifestyle

4. D – 55

5. A – The Sierra Nevada Range

6. C – 10

7. True

8. B – Mark Smith

9. D – All of the above

10. D – Wrangler

11. B – To tell drivers if their Jeep vehicles qualify for the trails.

12. C – 0

13. C – a more adult version of the Rubicon Trail Jamboree

14. False – While most are full, you can still get on the waitlists for almost every Jamboree.

15. A – Meals

16. B – Pets are highly discouraged at Jeep Jamborees.

17. A – No tires larger than 40″

18. True

19. D – If they ride in your Jeep.

20. C – Ten days prior to the event

DID YOU KNOW?

- Most Jamborees are family events, with some, such as the Rubicon Trail, having spin-off adult events, like Jeepers. This is a longer weekend for adults. There are also special family pricing plans available, instead of the per-person prices, to try to make it more affordable for families. This does not include the Rubicon Trail, however.

- Classic Jamborees include three meals on Friday and Saturdays for participants on weekend events. Select jamborees include evening meals only. Adventure Jamborees include zero meals. All participants are to do meals on their own.

- The Jeep rating system is a 1-10 scale, with only the Rubicon Trail having a rating of 10 and no trail actually having a 1. Most trails fit in the middle with ratings between 5 and 8.

- Practicing off-roading gives you a chance to hone the skills needed for various trails. But there are several things Jeepers should always do:

    1. Have a plan and be prepared. You should always have a buddy with you. Jeeping is supposed to be fun, and being with a buddy is absolutely more fun than bouncing around over rocks by yourself. If you have

kids, make sure there is one adult for every child in the Jeep. There should be no more than 4 people per Jeep in all. If you have two or more Jeeps, all the better!

2. You should have snacks and plenty of water. There is nothing worse than getting out there and being thirsty or hungry if something happens, like a flat tire or getting lost. A planned four-hour trip can actually take seven or eight hours if something should go wrong or you are just having an extra good time!

3. You should have a map and a full-sized spare. All Jeeps have a full-sized spare tire. Make sure it has air. Check your tools for a jack and other tools you might need. Tow straps are always a good idea.

4. Be sure and watch tire pressure over rocky areas as well as fluid levels in the engine.

5. Look ahead at the trail. This means look at the map and physically get out of your Jeep to actually look at the trail ahead to see what you are going to be doing in your Jeep. You will have more fun if you can mentally prepare for the road ahead!

- JJUSA (Jeep Jamboree United States of America) is the organization that plans and schedules all of the Jeep Jamborees across the nation and the world.

Originally founded by Mark Smith in 1982, this organization has continued to grow astronomically since that year. When Mark died in 2014, the entire Jeep world mourned his passing. Especially those who had participated in Jeep Jamborees felt a deep sense of loss. His family is still involved and carries on his legacy in the organization.

- There are now 700 staff members in JJUSA and almost 100 events across the United States and the globe involving Jeep. Pearce Umlauf is the current president and oversees operations. On top of his day-to-day operations, he also travels to visit remote areas in countries such as Kenya, Tanzania, Morocco, Vietnam, China, Peru, and various places in Europe to explore off-roading areas and to facilitate events.

- Shaun Gulling is the vice-president of operations and events. He has worked on over 100 Jeep Jamboree events and works with media to help with promotions of JJUSA. Shaun has also participated in the two-month expedition from Lima, Peru. This was a 20 year anniversary of part of Mark Smith's legendary ride, the "Expedicion de las Americas."

- Jake Horne is the director of registration for Jamboree events. Jake has a personal appeal much like Mark Smith. He travels to Jamboree events and interacts with participants on a regular basis. He loves to share the passion and excitement of off-roading with others.

- Rhiannon Murchie oversees the shipping and receiving of the organization. Because she has attention to detail, Rhiannon makes sure that items needed for JJUSA get to where they are needed when they are needed.

- Jim Horne started with JJUSA renting Jeeps to drivers and has worked in New Zealand to develop a significant trail and promotion program there for Jeep. He also works in the US on promotion for Jamborees.

- Ty Devereaux is the Adventure Consultant and Off-road Specialist for JJUSA. He has worked for the company for over 25 years, spending most of his time outdoors. He explores the trails and makes sure the ratings are correct. He also has completed a portion of the "Expedicion de las Americas" with Shaun Gulling.

CHAPTER 7:

JEEP OWNERS AND THE JEEPS THEY DRIVE

1. Jeep owners like to think of themselves as:

   a. People who love to own a Jeep and other brands.
   b. People who love to own one Jeep for the trail and another for the road.
   c. People who love adventure.
   d. People who are very careful with their vehicles.

2. What does the term "Mall Crawlers" refer to in reference to Jeep owners?

   a. Jeep owners who leave the doors on their Jeeps
   b. Jeep owners who use their Jeeps to shop at the mall
   c. Jeep owners who ride slowly on the trails
   d. Jeep owners who crawl up mountains with their Jeeps

3. Some people who own Jeeps are concerned about the famous Jeep "death wobble." What in the world is that?

    a. A Jeep has been driven too hard on the trails
    b. A Jeep is wobbly after a good trail ride
    c. A Jeep has a wobble in the seats
    d. A Jeep has damage to steering or suspension

4. When Jeep owners go off-roading, they should always bring:

    a. A flashlight
    b. Trail food, in case they get lost
    c. A snake bite kit
    d. A buddy

5. Jeep owners feel extra special because of:

    a. The Jeep wave
    b. The hidden Easter eggs
    c. Jeep Jamborees
    d. All of the above

6. The Jeep Community is the biggest in:

    a. Texas
    b. California
    c. The United States
    d. The world

7. Jeep owners love Jeeps because:

    a. They are easy to customize.
    b. They have a death wobble.

    c. Jeeps are only front-wheel drive.

    d. Jeeps are best if you stay on the road.

8. Jeep owners do what with paint?

    a. They do many changes to house paint colors.

    b. They tend to use neon a lot.

    c. They do nothing with paint.

    d. They save paint for other Jeep owners.

9. Jeep owners tend to take a lot of photos:

    a. Of their Jeeps

    b. Of their dogs

    c. Of their kids

    d. Of themselves

10. Jeeps, as a rule, get really good gas mileage which is great for their families. (T/F)

11. Jeep drivers also use:

    a. Trekking poles

    b. Selfie sticks

    c. Extra floor mats

    d. Extra brake shoes

12. Jeep owners know one thing:

    a. Jeep wave is kind of creepy, but they do it anyway.

    b. Jeeps are great for off-roading, but they do not last.

    c. If you take care of your Jeep, it can last 10-15 years.

d. Jeeps need their brakes replaced often.

13. Jeep drivers can name many reasons they buy a Jeep:
    a. The price
    b. Good all-weather vehicles
    c. Easy to drive
    d. All of the above

14. Jeep owners often join Jeep:
    a. Neighborhoods
    b. Clubs
    c. Jeepers
    d. Flashlight tag

15. The best Jeep is:
    a. Your Jeep
    b. The Rubicon
    c. The Wrangler
    d. The Cherokee

16. Because you own a new Jeep with no top or a soft top, you have to increase security. (T/F)

17. Fun Jeep life includes:
    a. Higher gas prices
    b. Repairs on Jeeps
    c. Jeep events
    d. All of the above

18. To be called a "Jeep girl" is:
    a. An insult.

b. Something funny.

c. A name that means you dinged your Jeep.

d. The ultimate compliment.

19. Men and women love to _____ their Jeeps.

    a. Wash

    b. Accessorize

    c. Change tires on

    d. Change windshield wipers on

20. New Jeep owners are surprised most by:

    a. The Jeep wave — why do so many people know them all of a sudden?

    b. Finding so many Jeeps parked beside theirs in the parking lot.

    c. The surprise Easter egg pictures in various parts of their vehicles.

    d. All of the above

ANSWERS

1. C – People who love adventure

2. A – Jeep owners who leave the doors on their Jeeps

3. D – A Jeep has damage to steering or suspension.

4. D – A buddy

5. D – All of the above

6. C – The United States

7. A – They are easy to customize.

8. B – They tend to use neon a lot.

9. A – Of their Jeeps.

10. False – Jeeps do not get good gas mileage.

11. B – Selfie sticks

12. C – If you take care of your Jeep, it will last 10-15 years.

13. D – All of the above

14. B – Jeep clubs

15. A – Your Jeep

16. True

17. C – Fun Jeep events

18. D – The ultimate compliment

19. B – Accessorize

20. D – All of the above

DID YOU KNOW?

- A Jeep owner is quoted as saying, "Owning a Jeep is like owning an airplane. You don't buy a plane to let it sit on the ground, you buy one to fly it. You don't buy a Jeep to just go to the mall. I mean, it doesn't have a seven-slot grill because seven is a lucky number. It is because Jeep was the first vehicle to drive on all seven continents." One can only guess what he or she meant in this quote, but adventure does come to mind.

- Jeeps as a rule are gas guzzlers, similar to their Hummer cousins. They are not nearly as bad as Hummers, but depending on the Jeep, it can take a good amount of gas to hit the trails the way many Jeepers want to do.

- Jeep has planned for the future, and you may be surprised to read, that Jeep is going electric and developing a hybrid model to combat the gas-guzzling reputation. Jeep is reaching out to protect the environment as well as their loyal followers' and future owners' pocketbooks at the gas pumps.

- There are Jeep clubs in every state. You can probably find one near where you live. This is such a great way to meet other Jeep drivers and possibly someone who wants to join with you on a trail ride or team up with you and your family. Jeep clubs are a great way to join the Jeep family and learn how to work on your Jeep as well as learn the tricks of trail riding.

- Jeep owners love being Jeep drivers. Jeeps park together in parking lots without knowing who they are parking next to. They are parking next to another Jeep, and that is good enough. It is not uncommon to see a line of Jeeps next to each other at a ballgame or the mall.

- People who drive Jeeps, as a rule, love to share their Jeep with family and friends. One of the rules of a Jamboree is that you cannot enter a Jamboree without a partner in the vehicle with you. This is for safety, but it is also for fun! And one of the rules of the off-road life is to never go off-roading alone. It just is not a good idea. Jeeping is a group activity, not a solitary endeavor. People come together to enjoy the passion of loving their Jeeps, their families, and the great outdoors!

- Jeep owners have a saying, "It's a Jeep thing," or an even more annoying saying: "You wouldn't understand. It's a Jeep thing."

- Jeep owners like to park on curbs or partially on sidewalks like they are off-roading in the city or something like that.

- Most Jeep owners also have a dog, but pets are discouraged on trails.

- Some Jeep owners are under the impression they are supposed to make their Jeeps look like futuristic war vehicles.

- Sometimes a Jeep owner might get overzealous. They may see an obstacle that even a Jeep should not tackle and end up needing help. That's what we have a buddy system! Two or three Jeeps are better than one.

- Jeep owners are as different as the Jeeps themselves, but at the same time, all Jeep owners are welcome in the Jeep family.

CHAPTER 8:

MORE JEEP WRANGLER... BECAUSE IT'S JEEP WRANGLER!

1. During what year were no Jeep Wranglers produced?

    a. 1993
    b. 1990
    c. 1996
    d. 1995

2. Jeep Wranglers have a "Trail Rated" badge on the:

    a. Wrangler's side.
    b. Wrangler's windshield in the corner.
    c. Wrangler's front grill.
    d. Wrangler's fender.

3. Why did the military fold down their windshields in the original Willys Wrangler Jeeps?

    a. They needed to see better.
    b. It helped to keep the windshield intact.

    c. They could fire their guns without standing up.

    d. It kept dust out of the cabin.

4. A proper Jeep Wrangler wave should be:

    a. Two fingers from the wheel at about 12:00.

    b. Both hands on the wheel and first two fingers raised up.

    c. Full-blown wave with the left hand.

    d. The left hand just raised from the wheel.

5. A Jeep Wrangler that is well cared for can last up to:

    a. 300,000 miles

    b. 300,000-400,000 miles

    c. 200,000 miles

    d. Less than 100,000 miles

6. Without the _____ you will not be able to drive as smoothly and safely over rough terrain.

    a. Lift winch

    b. Tow equipment

    c. Correct rims

    d. Bull bar

7. Why should you have grab handles in your Jeep Wrangler?

    a. Safety and stability

    b. Color accents

    c. Because they are so cool

    d. You don't really need them

8. Jeep Wranglers have a unique design:
   a. Front-wheel drive so you can go anywhere
   b. Square lights on the front, back, and sides
   c. Removable doors, removable top, and a fold-down windshield
   d. A smooth ride over rough trails

9. Most Jeep Wrangler owners and makers say you should not buy a Wrangler unless you plan to go off-road. (T/F)

10. One disadvantage of driving a Jeep Wrangler is:
    a. The Wrangler is mostly for off-roading.
    b. When you take the doors off you also lose the side mirrors.
    c. The Wrangler seats are difficult to protect.
    d. All of the above

11. The Jeep Wrangler actually had square headlights between what years?
    a. 1941-1950
    b. 1965-1970
    c. 2010-2020
    d. 1985-1995

12. The 2020 Wrangler Unlimited has features that include:
    a. A one-touch automatic roof
    b. A larger variety of colors
    c. Larger tires
    d. All new front-wheel-drive system

13. What is the advantage of buying a Jeep Wrangler?

    a. Exceptional resale value

    b. Low cost of ownership

    c. Parts are affordable and it's easy to repair

    d. All of the above

14. Jeep Wranglers were not called Wranglers before 1987. They were called_____.

    a. Jeeps

    b. GPs

    c. CJs

    d. Willys

15. Jeeping is:

    a. A bad idea

    b. A sport

    c. Not advised in a Wrangler

    d. Only for radicals

16. In 2015 on his visit to the United States, Pope Francis actually rode in a:

    a. White Jeep Wrangler

    b. Dark blue Jeep Wrangler

    c. Red Jeep Wrangler

    d. White Grand Cherokee

17. You should only buy a Jeep if:

    a. You need a car to get from one place to another.

    b. You have a sense of adventure.

c. You are driving young children around all the time.

d. Top-of-the-line safety and security features are important to you.

18. Owning a piece of Wrangler history is part of the fun of owning a Jeep Wrangler.

    a. Jeep Wrangler stems from a 35-year history.
    b. Jeep Wrangler stems from a 50-year history.
    c. Jeep Wrangler stems from a 25-year history.
    d. Jeep Wrangler stems from a 75-year history.

19. The Jeep Wrangler Rubicon is Jeep's improvement on:

    a. Style
    b. Trekking ability
    c. Comfort, room, and pick-up speed
    d. The price

20. A Jeep Wrangler is meant to be driven off-road, on trails, and near beaches. (T/F)

ANSWERS

1. C – 1996

2. D – Wrangler's fender

3. C – They could fire their guns without standing up.

4. A – Two fingers from the wheel at about 12:00

5. B – 300,000-400,000 miles

6. D – Bull bar

7. A – Safety and stability

8. C – Removable doors, removable top, and fold down windshield

9. True

10. B – When you take the doors off, you also lose the side mirrors.

11. D – 1985-1995

12. A – A one-touch automatic roof

13. D – All of the above

14. C – CJs

15. B – A sport

16. A – White Jeep Wrangler

17. B – You have a sense of adventure

18. D – Jeep Wrangler stems from a 75-year history.

19. C – Comfort, room, and pick up speed

20. True

DID YOU KNOW?

- Jeep Wranglers are meant to be enjoyed by people who love adventure and an element of freedom of the back roads. Jeep Wrangler is the icon of Jeeps and is meant to be driven off-road in such a way that it can tackle boulders, streams, hills, and valleys. Don't confuse streams with standing water. Jeep owners and people who help organize Jamborees and other trail rides always caution drivers against driving through deep standing or rushing water.

- The Jeep wave is common as is Jeep Wrangler owners parking together in mall parking lots. They may not know each other, but they know they are part of the club. Speaking of clubs, there are Jeep clubs all over the United States. In person and on social media, one can join a club in order to connect with others for adventure and fun driving the Jeeps.

- Jeep Wrangler owners have so many ways that they pay it forward. There are several charities they are involved in as a group. Jeepers in Galveston, Texas line up every year for a Suds run to benefit the Ronald McDonald House in the area. There may be several hundred Wrangler Jeeps in the line to drive a certain route in order to raise money for the Ronald McDonald House.

- Some Jeep clubs are organized for two purposes. One is for the purpose of connecting with other Jeepers, and two is to organize charity events. Jeep Wrangler clubs have been known to participate in the Susan B. Komen events every year, which raise money for Safe House battered women's shelter. Some also take on animal and pet causes. There have been various Jeep Wrangler clubs that have supported wildlife centers and pet adoption and food supply and shelter for unwanted animals. There are many clubs on Facebook.

- An attraction to the Jeep Wrangler is the ease with which owners are able to work on their own vehicles. Since WWII and the first model over 75 years ago, Jeep drivers have been able to use simple tools to work under the hood of their Jeep. Even now, parts are affordable and Jeep drivers say the work that is usually needed is pretty easy to do.

- The Jeep Wrangler is an iconic symbol of the Jeep. Being the closest model of the original Willys, this Jeep is the Jeep we all look to as the Jeep Brand model for what people expect when they see a Jeep on the trail. And rightly so. More people own Jeep Wranglers than any other model of the Jeep brand.

- The Jeep Wrangler has been known as a gas guzzler. However, the 2021 Jeep Wrangler Rubicon does get 29 mpg on the highway and 23 mpg in the city. This is much better than previous years of guzzling. This newer Jeep is a more comfortable ride as well.

- Jeep drivers also recommend covering the seats when you drive off-road. This will make cleaning much easier when you have finished a big day or weekend. Make sure they are washable seat covers. The seat covers truly do cover the entire seats of your Jeep. These are fully shaped to cover the entire front and back seats. Jeep owners can order these covers and will receive them within 2-3 days. It costs between $100-250 per full set of seat covers.

- The Jeep Wrangler has been written about and photographed almost as much as the original Willys.

- Today the Jeep Wrangler almost always lands in every Top 10 Off-road Vehicle list. No doubt it belongs near the top. The top of the line axles, shorter wheelbase, higher clearance, and flexible suspension make the Jeep Wrangler the off-road vehicle to reckon with.

- Not only are there several Jeep Renegade exterior colors, but there is also a Clear-coat option for those who want to add a sparkle to their vehicle.

Here are just a few of the Jeep Renegade exterior colors below. Let's find your favorite:

1. Black Clear-coat
2. Colorado Red Clear-coat
3. Alpine White Clear-coat
4. Bikini Metallic Clear-coat
5. Glacier Metallic Clear-coat
6. Granite Crystal Metallic Clear-coat
7. Jetset Blue Clear-coat
8. Omaha Orange Clear-coat
9. Slate Blue Pearl-coat
10. Sting-Gray Clear-coat

- Jeep Renegade has so many colors for your exterior, but don't forget about the Jeep Renegade interior colors. The Jeep Renegade interior colors combine to create a calming interior cabin. Jeep Renegade interior colors are black and ski gray black.

- The Jeep Wrangler is a fun convertible. It is a fun ride even if you are only riding around town. Coming soon in the near future for those who are willing to pay about four grand extra, the top can be automated rather than detachable. A flip of the switch and the top will move back while driving and viola, you will have an instant Jeep Wrangler convertible!

- Winter, Spring, Summer, or Fall...all you have to do is call and the Jeep Wrangler will be there because it is an excellent all-weather vehicle.

- Jeep Wranglers are able to be flat-towed, which means they can be towed with all four wheels down. If you have an RV or camper and want to tow your Jeep behind either of those, no worries, the handbook will show you how to easily set this up. The Jeep Wrangler is made to be on the move!

- Jeep may be making the Jeep Wrangler Rubicon have a half-door in the latter half of 2021. This Jeep has been seen being test-driven in various cities. They offer a much more airy and open feeling to the Wrangler than simply rolling the windows down. The half-door will enable you to completely remove the windows but keep the doors on if you want to keep the doors on. Most people want to take the doors completely off in a Wrangler. The half-door could add another option for drivers or families who want open air but not every side wide open. The Jeep does look pretty awesome with the windows off!

- If you are a Jeep Wrangler owner or love someone who drives a Jeep Wrangler, we have included a list of eight gifts every Jeep Wrangler owner would love to have:

1. A parking sign for their Jeep. Every Wrangler owner wants a specially designated place to park their ride. And a Jeep parking sign is the greatest gift for that.

2. A genuine leather, (but not bulky) key chain with the Jeep logo on the key chain.

3. A smaller version Jeep for the kids to have for their very own! What a great idea!

4. Jeeps are the perfect car for off-road trips and the great outdoors. Who doesn't need a bottle opener for their Jeep? This particular bottle opener is customized for Jeeps.

5. Jeep metal signs. They are all over Amazon and Etsy. Just do a sign check. Some are a pretty good size and a true Jeep lover will love one or more of these signs.

6. Jeep picture frames belong in the home of true Jeep fans. Just put the words in Google and you will have the cutest Jeep frames show up for the buying.

7. Jeep Blankets, water bottles, and seat covers are always great gifts for any Jeep owner.

8. A hand-held CB radio for those off-road excursions. We do not want our Jeep-loving friends to be completely disconnected from the rest of the world in case they run into

problems. A good hand-held CB radio runs about $100.

- Ten crazy things and fun to do with your Jeep Wrangler

    1. Even if you don't do the Jamboree, you should drive the Rubicon Trail.

    2. Rent a Jeep in Germany and drive the Autobahn. No speed limits allowed.

    3. Drive vertically up a wall with a winch. People who have done this say there isn't anything like looking out the windshield up at the sky and looking through the rearview mirror at the ground. It does take a level of bravery and being used to using the winch.

    4. Drive with the top down as much as you can!

    5. Take your Jeep tent and live in your Jeep for a while in the back country. Think of how long Mark Smith was on the open road when he drove from South America to the tip of Alaska. It was an almost seven-month trip! You can live in your Jeep for a couple of weeks and look at the stars a few nights.

    6. Rent a Jeep in an exotic place, such as an island paradise.

7. Paint your Jeep yourself. Watch YouTube! It might be a mess, but it's your Jeep Wrangler, so it's part of owning a Jeep, right?

8. Explore the back country in Colorado, California, South Dakota, Alaska, or any state for that matter. Just get off the main road in your Jeep Wrangler.

9. Definitely drive on the beach! But don't drive into the ocean!

10. Drive around on a snowy day with your tow rope and help people who are stuck. Or even better, attach a snowplow to the front of your Jeep and randomly plow for friends, relatives, and neighbors.

- Moab, Utah is a place Jeep Wrangler drivers mention in talking about scenic and challenging trail rides. Other than the Rubicon Trail, Moab, Utah has several trails that are highly recommended for Wrangler owners to try. The Moab area is one of the most challenging trail testing sites for Jeeps and this local area offers a rich 4x4 culture that welcomes Jeep drivers warmly from all over the country.

- Another Wrangler challenge that some drivers are taking is to map out cross-country trips where they only drive *roads less traveled*. One route is to jump on the old Highway 66. Still, others are mapping out even less traveled roads than discontinued highways.

- Drivers are starting on one coast or another and just taking back country roads East or West, depending on where they began. Talk about adventure! Of course, if you try something like that, you can be sure you are going to do some backtracking. Some kind of a map is warranted. Remember, the hood is a great place to study a map and make plans with your friends.

- Stargazing in your Jeep Wrangler takes on a whole new meaning. We suffer from light pollution in towns and cities, but the Jeep Wrangler takes care of that. The Wrangler can get your group away from the lights and in the back country in no time. You will get a starlight view like you have never seen before with the view from your Jeep Wrangler. The off-roads offer the best of day or night views.

- Another great ride is hitting the back country on the East Coast. Jeep drivers begin in the far North in Maine and drive South as the leaves turn so they can enjoy the beautiful Fall colors offered like nowhere else in this country. The Jeep Wrangler or any Jeep will allow a great view from Maine to Georgia.

- One piece of advice: if your Jeep is out of warranty, you should contact friends in your Jeep club or ask around on Facebook to find a good mechanic who can work on your Jeep Wrangler. You may want to do all the work yourself and it's good to know how to make simple repairs and modifications. However, you should have a mechanic you trust to work on your Jeep should something go wrong and you don't know how to fix the problem. With all vehicles an "ounce of prevention is worth a pound of cure" but a Jeep is not an ordinary vehicle. Jeeps go through a lot more than other cars. It stands to reason there are things that could and may go wrong during or after some of the off-roading adventures. Having a good, trusted mechanic is worth a pound of gold to help keep your Jeep running top-notch and ready for the next Jeep experience!

CHAPTER 9:

THE LARGER JEEPS

1. Which Jeep vehicle has won the most awards as an SUV?

    a. Jeep Compass
    b. Jeep Grand Cherokee
    c. Jeep Patriot
    d. Cherokee

2. The Jeep Compass has

    a. 4 wheel drive.
    b. Front-wheel drive.
    c. All-wheel drive.
    d. none of the above

3. Why buy a Jeep Gladiator?

    a. It is a great SUV crossover.
    b. It gets great gas mileage.
    c. It is the only convertible truck on the market.
    d. It has a long bed for hauling items.

4. The Jeep Cherokee has been around since which decade?

a. 1970s
b. 1960s
c. 1980s
d. 1950s

5. Which Jeep SUV sports a full V8 engine and is the best for long road trips on the highway?

a. Jeep Cherokee
b. Jeep Gladiator
c. Jeep Compass
d. Jeep Grand Cherokee

6. The most expensive SUVs to date, when certain options are added, top out with prices above

- $100,000

- $40,000

- $34,000

- $90,000

7. Jeep sales:

a. Plummeted in the last decade
b. Kept rising in the last decade
c. Stayed level in the last decade.
d. Rose exponentially in the last decade.

8. According to US News and World Report, the best-used car to buy is:

a. Jeep Cherokee
b. Nissan Pathfinder
c. Jeep Compass

d. Jeep Grand Cherokee

9. Jeep gives a bonus incentive of $500 if these people buy a Jeep:

    a. Teachers, doctors, and nurses
    b. Law officers, firefighters, EMTs
    c. Military
    d. Both b and c

10. The 2021 Jeep Compass:

    a. Is a gas guzzler.
    b. Gets over 30 mpg on the highway.
    c. Is a rough ride.
    d. Is a disappointment.

11. All Jeep SUV models share a common DNA because:

    a. They have authenticity.
    b. Jeep is the car that helped win WWII.
    c. Jeep is a rugged, reliable American-made car.
    d. All of the above

12. If a Jeep is a high-altitude vehicle, this means:

    a. The Jeep is able to cruise easier at high altitudes.
    b. The Jeep is set for high-altitude trails.
    c. The Jeep is a high-end luxury edition.
    d. The Jeep was manufactured at a higher altitude, so it runs smoother.

13. Overland is:

a. The name of a trail in Overland Park, Kansas.
b. Luxury trim for Grand Cherokee, Gladiator, and Cherokee
c. The name of a pass in the Ozarks.
d. The name of the new sunroof on the Gladiator.

14. Summit is:

a. Luxury trim for the Grand Cherokee with an over $50,000 price tag.
b. The top of a mountain
c. The end of the Colorado Jamboree for SUVs.
d. The name for the newest SUV hitting the market in 2022.

15. Jeep is celebrating 80 years in 2021, with:

a. A 4-star rated Jeep Gladiator.
b. A 5-star rated Jeep Grand Cherokee.
c. Adding eight new Jamborees. One for each decade!
d. A 5-star rated Jeep Cherokee

16. The larger Jeep SUVs:

a. Are allowed on the Rubicon Trail.
b. Do not allow many options.
c. Are great at taking off road.
d. Are difficult to obtain.

17. All Jeeps boast:

a. Less road noise than other brands.
b. Better traction than other brands.

c. More colors than other brands.

d. More mpg than other brands.

18. The Jeep Compass is considered a:

    a. Midsize SUV

    b. Full-size/premium SUV

    c. Compact SUV

    d. Crossover SUV

19. Of the larger SUVs, which Jeep is considered to be a full-size/premium SUV?

    a. Cherokee

    b. Grand Cherokee

    c. Renegade

    d. Compass

20. The Jeep Renegade is a Crossover SUV. (T/F)

ANSWERS

1. B – Jeep Grand Cherokee

2. C – All-wheel drive

3. C – It is the only convertible truck on the market.

4. A – 1970s

5. D – Jeep Grand Cherokee

6. A – $100,000

7. D – Rose exponentially in the last decade

8. A – Jeep Cherokee

9. D – Both B and C

10. B – gets over 30 mpg on the highway.

11. D – All of the above

12. C – The Jeep is a high-end luxury edition.

13. B – Luxury trim for the Grand Cherokee, Cherokee, and Gladiator

14. A – Luxury trim for the Grand Cherokee with an over $50,000 price tag

15. D – Adding a 5-star rated Jeep Cherokee

16. C – Are great at taking off road

17. B – Better traction than other brands

18. C – Compact SUV

19. B – Grand Cherokee

20. True

DID YOU KNOW?

- The new Jeep Trackhawk is said to be the ultimate Jeep Cherokee. The Trackhawk should almost be marketed as a race car. Give this car the open road, and it will show you what it can do. There are YouTube videos of Trackhawks racing each other on tracks. Racing aside, this car has a luxury-filled interior and exterior, with leather seating and modifications inside and sleek body-work on the outside. This SUV is trimmed out nicely as a true luxury SUV.

- In 2017, Jeep ranked 20th in reliability by Consumer Reports in SUV models. However, Jeep has improved and accessorized to the point that not only do the larger SUV models get better gas mileage, but the Grand Cherokee is considered to be a luxury vehicle with certain modifications. Jeep SUVs in 2021 are now ranked much higher by consumer reports, 5-star rated by customers, and number one by U.S. News and World Report.

- The Jeep Grand Cherokee is the most awarded SUV ever, and there are five reasons why this is a fact:

    1. **The safety features** in the Jeep Grand Cherokee are second to none in an SUV. There are over 70 available safety features

for owners to make the ride safer for their families. Every model has a standard feature of blind-spot monitoring complete with a rear-view camera system and a rear cross-path detection system. There are also adaptive safety features. They are rain-sensing windshield wipers, trailer sway control, and a backup trailer view camera. Also, an added feature includes a forward collision warning with an active brake system, adaptive cruise control with a stop mechanism, and parallel parking assist along with a perpendicular assist.

2. **The refined cabin** is unbeatable in the Jeep Cherokee. Of course, the Summit is going to bring the most luxury to the table, but any Cherokee does not disappoint. In the Summit, you will find leather accents along with leather seating. The first two rows are individual heated seats. All this is complete with a dual-zone climate control cabin.

3. **The power options** that Jeep offers in the Jeep Grand Cherokee are more than any other SUV model. The base is the 3.6-liter V6 engine with 295 horsepower. Another option is a 6.4-liter V8 engine with 475 horsepower. Also available is a 5.7-liter V8 with 360 horsepower. There are five options in total.

Rarely are there this many options for one model of car.

4. **The off-road capabilities** of the Jeep Grand Cherokee are outstanding. The Trackhawk model will take the off-road just as well as any smaller Jeep. This SUV will bring comfort to the open trail.

5. The Jeep Grand Cherokee has one of the best entertainment systems available today. The **UConnect Infotainment System** is far and above what the average driver is used to in other SUVs. This system comes with the Uconnect 4C Nav and is complete with an 8.4-inch touch screen. This works with Apple CarPlay and Android Auto.

- US News and World Report has named the 2018 Jeep Cherokee the best used car buy at the end of 2020.

- Driving a Jeep SUV sets you and your passengers up just a little higher than average above the road. A Jeep SUV will give you a smooth ride while you are able to see the layout of the road. There are other drivers out there who may not drive as well as you do, so it helps to see those people coming. Riding just a little higher is thought by some to be safer.

- The Jeep Compass is an SUV that is more city-friendly and at the same time promotes the Jeep's adventurous spirit. The compass is a smaller SUV but a great family car for in-town or on the back roads.

- Jeep offers camping in style by sleeping in a Jeep tent from JustforJeeps.com. This tent is a 10-foot-by-10-foot square tent. It includes a full rain fly, an overhead storage net, and inside pockets you can use as compartments for your supplies as well as the way it hooks up to your Jeep. The tent can be attached to the rear of your Jeep for more storage space. This tent retails for less than $400, and it is perfect for off-road camping!

CHAPTER 10:

THE FUTURE FOR JEEP

1. In 2022, Jeep is rolling out a new and improved SUV. It is called:

   a. The Jeep Grand Wagoneer
   b. The Jeep Rocket
   c. The Jeep Boeing
   d. The Jeep Legend

2. Another Jeep improvement is:

   a. The Wrangler will have an electric option.
   b. The Jeep Grand Cherokee will have a hybrid option.
   c. Solar stations are being installed along trails.
   d. All of the above

3. An official Jeep Museum is scheduled to open in 2022. It is going to feature:

   a. Current Jeeps
   b. Future of Jeep
   c. Jeep history and folklore
   d. Jeep drivers talking your ear off

4. At the rate Jeep is going, all vehicles may have an electric or hybrid version by:

   a. 2023
   b. 2024
   c. 2022
   d. 2025

5. If you buy a Jeep in 2021, how much of a future do you have with your Jeep?

   a. 15-20 years if you take care of it
   b. 10 years if you are lucky
   c. 5-7 years
   d. 6-10 years

6. What does taking care of your hypothetical future Jeep mean?

   a. No off-roading
   b. Regular maintenance
   c. Do not overload the Jeep
   d. Leave doors and roof on during rain

7. The Jeep wave has become:

   a. Annoying
   b. Something Jeep owners don't do anymore
   c. A full hand wave instead of 2 fingers
   d. A company symbol.

8. A future slogan for Jeep is:

   a. "We wave to everyone!"
   b. "Off-roading, here we go!"

c. "Online shopping. Driveway delivery."

d. "Forward, forward. Go, go, go!"

9. The Grand Wagoneer is a return to the old classic while adding:

    a. Luxury
    b. Extra tires
    c. More Easter eggs
    d. Seating for 5

10. If Jeep's goal was to have all-electric or hybrid options by 2022, they are on the way to making this goal. (T/F)

11. Jeep is _____ stepping into the future.

    a. Meekly
    b. Boldly
    c. Timidly
    d. Not

12. While Jeep moves into the future, the company does not forget its beginning 80 years ago.

    a. The first Jeeps were sold to Americans just before WWII.
    b. Jeeps were manufactured in 1941 for people to drive in England.
    c. Willys Jeeps were made for soldiers in WWII.
    d. The first Jeeps were made in the 1960s.

13. The new Compass has been previewed in

    a. The UK

b. France

c. Canada

d. China

14. The Jeep Grand Wagoneer has been named:

    a. Too expensive

    b. A high maintenance vehicle

    c. The best car to buy

    d. The car to steer away from

15. Before releasing the 2022 Jeep Grand Cherokee, Jeep will release:

    a. The new Compass

    b. Jeep Grand Wagoneer

    c. The electric Jeep Wrangler

    d. Jeep Grand Cherokee L

16. The new Jeep Wagoneer does not have something the older Wagoneer had:

    a. The wood paneling

    b. All-wheel drive

    c. Five doors

    d. The seven-slot grill

17. The future of Jeep makes Jeep one of FCA's most important brands. (T/F)

18. Jeep is making bold claims about"

    a. Its electric future.

    b. The new luxury line of SUVs.

    c. Charging stations on trails.

d. All of the above

19. Jeep dealers are mostly excited about:
    a. The electric Jeep Wrangler
    b. The new Jeep Grand Cherokee
    c. Selling used Jeeps
    d. The Jeep Grand Wagoneer

20. Jeep dealers are excited about selling used Jeeps because Jeeps are cheap and do not retain their value if they are used. (T/F)

ANSWERS

1. A – The Jeep Grand Wagoneer

2. D – All of the above

3. C – Jeep history and folklore

4. C – 2022

5. A – 15-20 years if you take care of it.

6. B – Regular maintenance

7. D – A company symbol

8. C – "Online shopping. Driveway delivery."

9. A – Luxury

10. True

11. B – Boldly

12. C – Willys's Jeeps were made for soldiers in WWII.

13. D – China

14. C – The Best Car to Buy

15. D – Jeep Grand Cherokee L

16. A – Wood paneling

17. T – True

18. D – All of the above

19. C – Selling used Jeeps

20. False

DID YOU KNOW?

- The 2022 Grand Wagoneer is scheduled to debut in the Spring of 2021. This is a return to the family wagon but with so many luxury improvements. To begin, this Jeep has three rows of seats, and this car will be featured in the Premium SUV line of the Jeep models. The sticker price will begin between $60,000 and $70,000. Fully loaded, the Jeep Grand Wagoneer prices out above $100,000. One feature buyers will surely want is a single pane tinted glass-top the length of the entire vehicle for either nighttime star gazing or daytime views. The rest we will know closer to the first official viewing.

- The next surprise in Jeep's future is an all-electric Jeep Wrangler. There are also plans to install solar power charging stations along the Badge of Honor trails in the five-year Jeep plans. The Grand Cherokee will also have a plug-in feature option if buyers want to purchase a hybrid Grand Cherokee.

- The new Wrangler 4xe is coming in with a bang to lead the smaller Jeep SUVs. The manufacturer's estimation puts the 4xe at 50 mpg, which is almost twice the Jeep Wrangler gas model's rating. This electric Jeep also has a range of 400 miles. There are not many trails you can't conquer with a full charge! After you finish, you can go home, plug it back in, and recharge for the next time you hit the streets or the trail!

- Jeep owners can have a great future with any Jeep. But the record shows, you must take care of your vehicle. This does not mean to just drive it on the streets. No. This means to get the oil changed and do the regular service and repairs needed on your Jeep. Learn the correct ways to do off-roading, and then go! Jeeps were made to go off-road. You have to know how to lift your car and what size wheels are needed for what trail you are on. Join a club, and make friends with other Jeepers. Then you will not only learn how to drive off-road, but you will learn how to work on your own Jeep. They are easy to work on. YouTube is your friend, but so is the Jeeper in your club. Enjoy your Jeep, but take care of it. Clean it up after a good trail ride. Get washable seat covers, then do not worry about the rest. The Jeep was made to get dirty and wet. It's ok. Enjoy the adventure!

- The Jeep wave has become a company symbol and a customer care motto. They state that "Every new Jeep brand vehicle now includes the best-in-class coverage of Jeep wave customer care." This includes worry-free maintenance. What worry-free maintenance means is that there is no mileage limit, and your Jeep has 24/7 support, discounts, and access to VIP events.

- The Principal Chief of the Cherokee Nation has requested Jeep stop using the name Cherokee on their vehicles. This was announced in February 2021. Jeep responded by saying, "We are committed to an open and respectful dialogue with Cherokee Nation Principal Chief Chuck Hoskin, Jr."

- While car dealers are extremely excited to see the new Jeep Grand Wagoneer, they still love to sell used Jeeps. Used Jeeps are still a big part of the future of Jeeps and the future for Jeep owners. A used Jeep to one person may be a new Jeep to another person. Each new person or driver finds their Easter eggs and is ready for new experiences with their Jeep. For Jeep drivers, the future of Jeep begins when you turn the key in your Jeep!

- What should you do if you decide to go with the idea of buying a used Jeep instead of a Jeep off the showroom floor? Buying a used Jeep can be an excellent choice, but buying a used Jeep is very different than buying a different brand of any other used car. There are some specific things you need to check before you make a purchase because you have to assume the Jeep has been used to go off-roading at some point by the last driver.

- Most Jeeps should have skid plates underneath their body if they have been used for off-roading. You are going to have to go under the Jeep to see the skid plates and what they look like. You can tell if they have been recently replaced or what kind of shape they are in. If the Jeep has been used in lots of off-roading, things will look pretty beat up underneath. Or you can notice if the skid plates have been replaced or repainted. Depending on how the underneath looks, this Jeep may have more wear and tear than you may want to have for your new used car.

• There may be extra modifications on a used Jeep you are interested in. You should check the suspension because normally that is where many modifications happen first. The best advice is to only buy a modified Jeep if you are going to off-road or truly like what has been done. Otherwise, stay with an unmodified Jeep.

• The tires are more important on a Jeep than perhaps another vehicle. Because the Jeep should be able to handle any situation in which you will drive, you want the tires to be in good condition and the correct tires for the vehicle in question. Check for uneven wearing, too much on one side or another, or even down just the middle. This could indicate an alignment problem. Compare the front to the back tires. If the front are more worn down than the back, this is an indicator that the tires were not rotated properly. You don't want to buy a Jeep and then have to replace the expensive tires right away. Plus, the tires will indicate to you there are other problems as well.

- Checking for rust is super important on any model and brand of vehicle. You do not want a rusty Jeep. If the Jeep you are looking at has rust, it very possible it has crossed a stream and water has seeped into places and not dried properly. It probably has had repeated exposures to water and mud and was not cared for properly. Back away from the vehicle.

- Check for leaks. A good trick when looking for any car is to look on a dry day. This makes it much easier to check for leaks from the engine. Look where the Jeep is parked when you pull away from the spot. Any number of things can cause a Jeep engine or hose to spring a leak, from a loose rock on the trail to a hose coming loose after several rough rides. Check extra closely when looking under the hood.

- Buying a used Jeep is a great idea if that is the way you decide to go, but make sure you have dotted all of your i's and crossed all of your t's when checking the used car lot for Jeeps. Don't just fall in love with the shiny new color and the promise of adventure without doing a thorough check.

CONCLUSION

After participating in Jeep Trivia and reading information about 80 years of Jeep history and various Jeep highlights and facts, the average reader might be running to the nearest Jeep dealer! It would be hard to read of all the fun and adventure without wanting to join in on the excitement. It seems that anyone who is not a member of a Jeep club is truly missing out on something special.

This Trivia Book is designed to bring tons of facts and details about the Jeep brand. From the beginning of Jeep, through the 80 years of the development of Jeep, and all the adventures in between, Jeep is an icon that is here to last!

This book brought you the history, current events, and future of Jeep within over 50 pages of questions, answers, and facts. This has been for enjoyment and to strengthen your knowledge of Jeep and every car they have made and are going to make in the near future.

At first glance, the Jeep Wrangler would offer the freedom to live a life of adventure and have fun on the trails. A bucket list item would be to drive the Rubicon trail and to participate in the Rubicon Jamboree. If a

Wrangler is not your style, there are any number of Jeeps you can drive off-road. All Jeeps are currently suited to drive off-road.

In 2022, when the new Wagoneer is released and someone spends over $100,000 on this car, it is up to that owner if they want to off-road with this vehicle. However, rest assured, this will be one vehicle that will not get stuck in the snow or be stopped by a small stream or any normal back road. You could vacation in this vehicle and hit the back roads without a worry. Would I take such a car and hit a #8 Jamboree trail ride on purpose? No, but I would not hesitate to take this car on back roads in Colorado, South Dakota, California, or other scenic places in order to get my family in the back country to experience scenic routes other cars cannot experience.

Driving a Jeep is about the experience. It's about the possibility of more: more adventure, more connections with others, and more freedom to discover nature. Jeepers get it. It's like flying. It's like riding a bicycle, only faster. Bicycles can go places cars cannot go. And so do Jeeps. Jeeps go places other cars cannot go. People who drive Jeeps get to experience places in this country that other people never see unless a Jeep driver or passenger will take photos and share them with those less fortunate.

One has to wonder about the history of Jeep. If WWII hadn't happened, would we still have the Jeep? It would seem the cards had to line up just right at the right time for this icon to be created. And for a car developed for soldiers to translate back to civilians and catch on in such a way, the brand would last 80 years and is still going strong with a bright future.

In many ways, we owe a debt of freedom to the Jeep. The Jeep was a loyal fighter in WWII on the field with our troops on the roads, on the beaches, and even dropped from the air to go into battle. Jeeps were there to do their job.

In a way, this set the tone for the next life of Jeep and the direction manufacturers of Jeep would go. Jeep persevered when other automakers did not. Jeep rose above problems and setbacks and came back even stronger than before. With the Jeep Wrangler leading the way, Jeep expanded into the SUV market and began leading the way on the trail and the road!

The community of Jeep is a large factor in the success of the investment of Jeep. Mark Smith started the first Jeep Jamboree across the Rubicon Trail. This one trail ride began a yearly event that grew into several national and worldly Jamborees. These events grow every year and help start more Jeep clubs for more members. Jeep is the one brand that is a community. Jeep is family.

If you buy a Jeep, you are automatically included because everyone recognizes a fellow Jeep driver on the road. It is impossible to not recognize the seven-slot front grill. And once you start to look for other Jeeps on the road and parking lots, you begin to see more and more Jeeps.

Jeeps are easy to work on. From the Jeeps on the battlefields to the Jeeps in your driveway, drivers are able to work on their own Jeeps if they just give it a try. Parts are inexpensive, and there are any number of YouTube videos to watch as demonstrations as to how to fix certain things on your Jeep. Also, if you are a member of a Jeep Club, people help each other out. Jeep people truly are a community.

As we have read in this Jeep trivia book, Jeep is a household name and a car that is easily recognized coming down the road. What started in WWII with Jeep working to help soldiers win the war has now developed into several models of the same Jeep brand. What a terrific history and story the Jeep has that no other automotive company can boast. This is a unique, one-of-a-kind brand.

If you take time to sit back and think about every Jeep Jamboree and every Jeep club, you can scarcely take it in. The influence and impact Jeep has had the last 80 years has been a testament to the progress of our society. You can see the progress of the United States reflected in the Jeep brand itself. From Willys to the Trackhawk and back to the Wrangler again, the Jeep represents who we are or the best of who we would like to be.

Jeep takes us to our roots of exploration and the open trail. Finding out what is the next bend and being out in the open air are the very reasosn we are drawn to Jeep life. From the Easter eggs to the modifications coming in 2022, owning a Jeep is an experience that Jeep owners understand. If you love a Jeep, you love adventure. It's a Jeep thing.